The Last Resort

Chris Owen

Series editor Rob Brannen

Hodder &

A MEMBER OF THE H

For My Mum

Performance Rights

All rights whatsoever in these plays are strictly reserved, and professional applications and amateur applications for permission to perform them, etc., must be made in advance before rehearsals begin, to: Lucy Johnson, Hodder and Stoughton Educational, English and Drama Department, 338 Euston Road, London NW1 3BH.

The songs mentioned within the play are suggestions only. You might want to choose other songs for your performance. The publishers of this book do not accept any responsibility for the copyright of songs. Performances should apply to the individual record company for performance rights.

Song Reference (in order of use)
'The Good, the Bad and the Ugly' by Enio Morricone, 'Wake up' by the Boo Radleys, 'Road to Nowhere' by Talking Heads, 'Always Look on the Bright Side of Life' by Monty Python, 'Young at Heart' by The Bluebells, 'Albatross' by Fleetwood Mac, 'The Boys are Back in Town' by Thin Lizzy, 'Girls Just Wanna Have Fun' by Cyndi Lauper, 'I'm Too Sexy', by Right Said Fred, 'Guaglione' by Perez Prado, 'Ride on Time' by Black Box, 'Surfin USA' by The Beach Boys, 'Wipe Out' by the Surfaris, 'Justified and Ancient' by The KLF, 'You Took the Words Right Out of My Mouth' by Meatloaf, 'Get Ready For This' by 2 Unlimited, 'Celebration' by Kool and the Gang, 'You Get What You Give' by New Radicals.

Orders: please contact Bookprint Ltd, 130 Milton Park, Abingdon, Oxon OX14 4SB. Telephone: (44) 01235 827720, fax: (44) 01235 400454. Lines are open from 9.00—6.00, Monday to Saturday, with a 24 hour message answering service. You can also order through our website www.hodderheadline.co.uk

British Library Cataloguing in Publication Data
A catalogue record for this title is available from The British Library

ISBN 0 340 77686 2

First published 2001
Impression number   10 9 8 7 6 5 4 3
Year   2007 2006 2005 2004

Cover photo © Corbis Images
Typeset by Fakenham Photosetting Limited, Fakenham, Norfolk.
Printed in Great Britain for Hodder & Stoughton Education, a division of Hodder Headline, 338 Euston Road, London NW1 3BH by CPI Bath.

CONTENTS

INTRODUCTION

The Last Resort is a comedy ideally suited to any company seeking a youthful and fresh piece which places the emphasis firmly on the artistic skills of the cast. It features multiple role playing and an exaggerated and highly physical performance style. It should be of particular appeal to youth theatres, student companies, and senior school pupils.

It calls for an open and flexible staging. The cast can be almost any number from four upwards but in its original form was performed by a cast of twelve (six female, six male). Although there are clear male and female roles many of these can be interpreted effectively by the opposite gender.

This version of *The Last Resort* is based on the original production which was performed by Magnetic North Youth Theatre in Hillingdon and subsequently by BTEC students from Amersham and Wycombe College of Further Education at the Edinburgh Festival.

The Last Resort allows for:

1. a variable size cast with the desirability of multiple role playing.
2. through the use of multiple roles, the ability to create balanced roles for all performers.
3. the understanding of research into the roles and situations depicted.
4. flexibility in the realisation of areas of the script with responsibility given to individual performers.
5. exciting and risk taking physical theatre and the inclusion of elements of movement and mime.
6. an ensemble performance and the creation of a strong group identity.

Performance Exercises are included at the back of the text to kick-start the performance project.

LIST OF CHARACTERS

The Chorus

Vic (Clint) Eastwood
Woman (2)
Mugger
Landlady
Man

The Brews Up Posse:
Bobby Brewster DJ
Winnie Wurzel
Mr Scream
Frances Fairweather

Nellie Crabtree
Mr Minesweep

The Killjoy Family:
Wayne
Sharron
Carrie
Damien

The Bright Family:
Ray
Rosy
Hope
Sonny

Dawson's Donkeys:
Eric
Norbert
Stan

Old Ladies:
Betty
Dot
Mavis

Jackie

The Seagulls (4)

The Boys:
Brian
Darren
Jason
Kevin

The Girls:
Cheryl
Karen
Mandy
Tina

The Puppet Show:
Roberta
Shirley
Punch
Judy
Mr Policeman
The Crocodile
The Children

The Surfers:
Matt
Fraser
Clive

The Boyracers (2)

The Bouncers:
Psycho
Homerun

Mrs Higgins

The Last Resort

A practically bare stage except for some typically summery patio chairs around the sides and back of the stage. A lone saxophone plays 'Summertime' by Gershwin as the cast enter dressed in shorts and beachwear.

Chorus   All is quiet
All is still
In these last smooth soft moments of grey
    Just before the dawn.
    Beneath opaque sheets
    Snug and warm
    Lies the town
    Ferry Town
    Ferryton-on-Sea.
    Safe beneath its blanket of cloud it lies
    Still, silent, no movement
    But its breath can be heard
    The velvet crush of the waves
    As they caress the beach and withdraw
    Hush and you can hear it
Listen
    Listen
The town's breath.

The chorus creates the sound of three waves breaking on the beach

    Ferry Town
Every town
From Blackpool to Brighton
    From Cleethorpes to Clacton
    From Bournemouth to Bognor
    From Skegness to Southend
    From Margate to Morecombe
    From Torquay to Tenby
    From Weymouth to Yarmouth
    From Newquay
To Weston super Mare!
    The great British resort

Lies sleeping
But this is Ferryton-on-Sea

Pause

The Last Resort.
Listen

Another wave breaks on to the beach

Through clouds of summer
Strive to see
Thrusting into the ocean
. . . the sea
. . . well estuary
The mighty cliffs at one end of the bay
The lush green turfed headland at the other
The bull's horns that guard
The long, sweeping expanse of Ferry Town's glory
– the beach!
From which projects
In pale imitation of nature
That artificial, Victorian, folly
The Grand Pier.
On girdered legs, it strides out
Ankle deep in mud.
Behind the beach
But parallel
Runs the prom
The promenade!
Now deserted
No movement apart from
The wind blown,
Sand swept,
Chip paper
On the run from the beach lawns
Or the park
Or the Wintergarden.
But not for long
For Ferryton
The Last Resort

Is waking.
Hear it stir.

Pause

Eight streets back from the sea front lies Grosvenor
Road.
Along which comes the electric hum of the morning's
first milk float.
In the front of which,
Anoraked and waterproofed against the English summer,
Sits Mr Eastwood
Vic Eastwood.
Known to his friends,
And to himself in his fantasies,
As Clint.

A burst of the theme music from The Good, The Bad and The Ugly

Now a man alone, in the silent streets, half awake, half
asleep. Lost in his imagination he lives the perfect
milkman's dream.
A man who women would die for
And who men respect
Who can silence barking dogs . . .

Dogs bark

. . . with a glance.

The dogs whine pitifully

With a graceful leap he dismounts and approaches the
first door.

Woman	Oh Clint – it's you
Vic	(*as 'Clint'*) Yeah it's me. What can I do for you?
Woman	The usual will be fine.
Vic	I've no time for that – but I can leave you some milk.
Woman	Semi-skimmed?
Vic	Or full cream?
Woman	What about some . . .
Vic	Gold top?

Woman	Oh Vic.
Vic	And some yoghurt?
Woman	Oh Vic . . . look out!
Mugger	OK milky – hand over your cash.
Vic	You're up a little early ain't you sonny?
Mugger	Just let me have it.
Vic	Well, since you asked.

There is a brief struggle. The mugger is floored. He draws a gun. Vic draws a shotgun

Vic	Go ahead punk, make my day.
Mugger	OK – you've made your point.
Vic	Get out of here.
Woman	You sure can handle yourself.
Vic	Delivering milk is a man's business.
Woman	You're sure you won't stay?
Vic	I've got a round to deliver – sorry.
Woman	I'll never forgive you.
Vic	Then I'll just have to be . . . unforgiven – so long.
Chorus	But reality is not so generous.
Landlady	Here, Eastwood you good for nothing. You've left one pint short again. Don't bother looking for a Christmas bonus round here.
Man	Oi Eastwood, can't you make less noise? Some of us are trying to get some sleep. What do you have to come round so early for anyway?
Woman 2	If I catch you looking in my windows again, my Des will sort you out. You bloomin' pervert.
Chorus	With a sigh, Vic shakes the dog off his foot, gets back on his milk float, and soon the lulling hum of the motor takes him back to his dreams.

Music from The Good, The Bad and The Ugly as scene fades

	And like cracking an egg into a frying pan, the sun

twitches back the curtain of clouds and bursts
through to peer down onto Ferryton-on-Sea.
And with a sizzle of spitting fat.
Full English breakfast just £1.75
With fruit juice £2.50
Continental breakfast . . .?
What's that?
Ferryton stirs into life.
And at the flick of a switch, Bobby Brewster, the early
morning DJ on West Coast Radio.
The voice of the West Country.
Swings into action.

Bobby   Good morning listeners. It's Bobby Brewster and the
'Brews Up' posse (*whoops and assorted noises from the 'posse'*)
bringing you another thrill packed morning show
here on . . .

Jingle   West, West, West Coast Radio.

West, West, West Coast Radio.

The Voice of the West Country.

Bobby   Well isn't it looking great today gang? (*Whoops of
agreement*) Just to be sure let's get a word from one of
our favourite 'Brews Up' characters, Winnie Wurzel
the West Country Weather Woman. (*Whoops*) Winnie?

Winnie   Ah Bobby. Roight. Oi've chacked on my seaweed and
ee do be noice and droy. That there indicating loike
that it do be goin' a be a hot one today all roight. Any
old clouds on the coast will bugger off quick leavin'
clear skoys and that hot zun will be on uz all day. Zo
that's a top day all roight. So watch out you don't
fardle yer lallies by not covering yerself up. It's a straw
hat warning today! (*Singing*) Oh I got a brand new
combine harvester you got a brand new key . . .

Singing continues

Bobby   It seems the summer has finally arrived and it looks
like its going to be a bit of a scorcher . . . thank you
Winnie . . . thank you Winnie. (*Losing the 'Brews Up'
persona for a moment*) You can stop now. (*Singing stops*)

	These cider drinkers eh. Well the fine weather will be welcomed by all those early morning joggers, walkers and wacky characters down on Ferryton seafront. So if you're tuned into us on your walkman ...
Mr Scream	(*shouting*) Aaaaaaaghhh!
Bobby	No no. Back in your cage Mr Scream. This one is for you.

Music: Wake Up. Assorted joggers, dog walkers, tramps, people doing T'ai Chi, litter the stage eventually resolving into the very odd Nelly Crabtree (madwoman) and Mr Minesweep.

Nelly	Rubbish, that's what it is to them, rubbish. Just throw it away. They don't care.
Minesweep	(*sweeping the area with a metal detector*) Beep! (*Pause*) Beep! (*Pause*) Beep!
Nelly	Here, what you doin' of?
Minesweep	(*not hearing her*) Beep!
Nelly	Oi! You! Mr!
Minesweep	Beep!
Nelly	Oi! Can you hear me?
Minesweep	Beep, beep beep, beep beep beeeep!
(*He starts to dig*)	
Nelly	Oi! What you doin'?
Minesweep	Well – actually – I'm trying to dig up something. Just a minute. Here we are. Oh dear just another bottle top.

He throws the top away. Nelly scurries after it and retrieves it.

Nelly	Don't you want it then?
Minesweep	Well, I was hoping for something a little more valuable. Fifty pence perhaps.
Nelly	Well don't look at me. I've got nothing. So don't you mug me.
Minesweep	No, no – of course not. It's my metal detector. It finds metal things for me and I dig them up.
Nelly	You likes doin' that do you?

Minesweep	Oh yes. It can be jolly exciting. The sheer thrill of it. The anticipation as you walk along – not knowing what you might find. Digging here, digging there. Walking along. And I don't get cold. This anorak is jolly windproof I can tell you.
Nelly	I can find treasure without one of they things. Look I found this. Do you know what it is?
Minesweep	Well, I'm no expert but it does look after like a tail pipe off a car's exhaust.
Nelly	See – I might find the rest later. Then I'll be rich then.
Minesweep	Er yes.

Music – back to Bobby Brewster

Bobby	And that was (*insert song title here*). Now with the time fast approaching eight thirty it's time for a traffic update from our eye in the sky, the heroine of the hover, Frances Fairweather.
Frances	Well hello Bobby!
Bobby	Hi Frances! How are the roads looking?

In the background the chorus beat their chests to create the sound of the helicopter.

Frances	Well, fairly clear locally at the moment but there is already a lot of congestion on the motorways heading our way. In fact we have reports of ten mile tailbacks on the south bound carriageway of the M5. Unfortunately, a lorry carrying adhesives has shed its load.
Bobby	You could say it's a sticky situation.
Frances	Yes **you** could.
Bobby	Thanks a lot Frances. Catch you again later. Ten mile tail backs eh listeners. Still if you are marooned on the motorway, you can always tune into . . .
Jingle	West, West, West Coast Radio.
Bobby	So just sit back, and take it easy because it looks like you're on a *Road to Nowhere*.

Music: Road to Nowhere. The scene changes to the Killjoys stuck in the traffic jam listening to the car radio.

Wayne	God they do talk some tripe on these local radio stations.
Damien	Dad, are we there yet?
Wayne	How the hell can we be there! We've been stuck in this traffic jam for the last hour.
Damien	Can we go home then?
Wayne	We can't piggin' well go anywhere until we get past this lorry can we.
Carrie	Will you wind the windows down. It's boilin' in here.
Sharron	Well make up your mind will you. Last time you said you wanted them closed cause of the exhaust fumes.
Carrie	Well **now** I want them open.
Sharron	Alright then. Did you bring your swimmin' costume?
Carrie	What for? I'm not goin' on the beach. Sun's bad for ya ya know.
Wayne	Right little ray of sunshine you are. Dressed in black from head to foot. Hey, and put the head back on the noddin' dog on the rear window will ya. Looks stupid like that.
Carrie	When are we going to get to Ferryton? This is borin'.
Sharron	I thought you weren't interested in going to the seaside.
Carrie	I'm not. Local swimming pool's better.
Wayne	But it's not natural is it. The seaside is natural.
Carrie	Since when has natural had anything to do with it? The girls in those magazines you buy, are not very natural are they? All that silicone bouncing about. Would you prefer them to be more 'natural'?
Wayne	What a way to talk to your own father. You haven't been the same since you started going to that college, you haven't.
Damien	What magazines are these dad?
Wayne	You shurrup and have another mini roll.
Sharron	He's had five already. Just you watch that you don't be sick. And what magazines exactly are these Wayne?

Wayne	It's just something she's saying love. I haven't any magazines.
Sharron	You'd better not. You know what I think of that filth.
Carrie	Look under the socks in his dressing table if you don't believe me.
Wayne	Oh, **those** magazines!
Sharron	So you admit it then.
Wayne	Those are just some magazines that I borrowed off a mate at work.
Sharron	And that makes it alright does it?
Wayne	They're only copies of *Amateur Photographer*. I wanted to look something up.
Sharron	But we haven't got a camera!
Wayne	Well, that's just it. I was going to buy you one as a surprise but it's all ruined now.
Damien	Can I have a look at them magazines Dad?
Wayne	You wouldn't understand them Damien. They're very . . . 'artistic'.
Sharron	'Ere Wayne, when you gonna get these stickers sorted out. I'm fed up of people thinking I'm called Tracey.
Carrie	Isn't Tracey, the name of the Barmaid at the 'Swill and Bucket'?
Wayne	Carrie, don't you go stirrin' it. Oh God, me furry dice are fallin' off now.
Damien	Are we there yet?
Wayne	I'm gonna swing for that kid I swear it.
Sharron	Eh look, we're up to the bloomin' lorry at last. Should be clear soon.
Carrie	What's all that gunge all over the road? Oh it was carryin' glue.
Damien	Gi' us a look. Wind your window down dad.

Damien sniffs the air

Wayne	Eh enough of that. I don't know. What a family eh. Bloody drug addict you'll be.
Carrie	We could have avoided all this you know if we hadn't come on the motorway. We should have gone on minor roads like I said.
Damien	No services on minor roads are there. What are you supposed to do without services?

The scene switches to the Bright family parked and picnicking in a lay-by.

Rosy	Right come along everyone. The sandwiches are ready.
Ray	Yes, coming dear. Children!
Sonny	Here I am Father. I say it was jolly interesting looking at the cows in the field. Super fun.
Hope	I'm afraid I put my foot in a cowpat – poohey!
Rosy	Have you cleaned yourself up?
Hope	Of course I have, Mummy.
Ray	Now sit down and tuck in.

Chorus make an 'Eeeeeow' sound as a car goes past. The Brights watch and track the car in unison.

Sonny	It's super isn't it, just sitting here in the lay-by watching the traffic go past.
Ray	All thanks to the modern miracle of the compact folding chair.
Rosy	Where would we be without them.
Ray	Where would we be indeed!

Another car goes past

Hope	Lovely sandwich, Mummy.
Sonny	Yes it's terrific. Fish paste – my favourite!
Ray	You know, the seaside will be nice but it's hard to beat this.
Rosy	I know what you mean. Squash anyone?
Ray	Actually, I've got lots of room!
Sonny	I say, father's made a joke!

They all laugh

Hope   Well done daddy. Ripping.

Rosy   Super.

Another car passes and we switch to the chorus.

Chorus   Now, back to Ferryton prom, where, as the joggers
                  and dog walkers fade into semi-detached shade, the
                  sea front blossoms new life.
                  Multicoloured umbrellas bloom, and inflated
                  dinosaurs, hammers and bananas squabble, gibbeted
                  under shop front awnings.
                  Trestle tables, bowing under the weight of a thousand
                  beach balls, buckets and spades, Frisbees, windbreaks,
                  bats and Ferryton rock groan onto the pavement.
                  Postcards on whirling carousels, shiver in anticipation
                  of mysterious journeys to hidden homes.
                  (*As if reading a postcard*) 'Dear Eric and Carol, Well here
                  we are. B&B OK, landlady a bit of a dragon. Weather
                  and food OK. Frank and I still not talking but at least
                  it gives us something different to look at. Love from
                  Rita and the kids.'
                  Toffee apples spin and the candy floss machine whirls
                  its premiere pink blur.
                  Burners burst into flame, and in vats of glutinous fat
                  the first chips of the day simmer.
                  And by the pier, we pause to observe the arrival of
                  one of Ferryton's must illustrious attractions –
                  Dawson's Donkeys!

Music: 'Always Look on the Bright side of Life'. *The donkey's face the
audience. Each wears an appropriate hat complete with a name band. The donkey's name
bands are not the same as their character names.*

Stan   By heck, it's gonna be a hot one today Norbert.

Norbert   Happen your right there, Stan. Gonna be a hot one.

Eric   Crowds of bloody kids then.

Norbert   Loads of work for us.

Stan   I hate bloody kids me.

Eric	Pullin' me tail.
Stan	Kickin' us in't sides.
Norbert	And giddee up this, giddee up that.
Eric	I'd like to give them bloody giddee up.
Stan	And I've got the wrong hat on.
Norbert	What's it say then?
Stan	Flash! What sort of a name is that fer a donkey eh?
Eric	I was Flash t'other day. Always get the hyperactive ones on board when they call you Flash. Reckon yer a bloody Derby winner they do.
Stan	Well thanks for cheerin' us up Eric. That's really made my day.
Norbert	You think you've got problems. I'm called Daisy. Bloomin' girls name that.
Stan	Well if you get excited lookin' at Jenny again, there won't be much doubt will there.
Eric	Source of great entertainment that were. All the little kids pointing and asking their mums what the matter was with you.
Stan	Some interestin' answers there I felt!
Norbert	Alright, alright. Still look at the fetlocks on her eh! Who needs a carrot, just get her in front of me and . . .
Eric	(noticing Norbert is getting 'excited') Steady, steady!
Norbert	(checking himself and noticing too) Oh . . . right.
Stan	I see the sea's in at present.
Eric	Well, first lot we get – give 'em a drenchin' eh!
Stan	Agreed.
Norbert	Ah, I could do with a cold plunge me.
Stan & Eric	(in agreement) Aye!
Eric	I love to hear 'em scream when they think we're out of control.
Stan	Bet, half of tonight's feed that I can buck more off today than either of you.

Norbert	Reckon, I'll take thee up on that Stan.
Eric	Me too.
Stan	Right, roll on the first victims then.
Norbert	Now there's a novel thought!

They burst into braying laughter. Scene switches to Frances Fairweather. Helicopter sounds

Frances	Time for my last report of the morning Bobby. With it coming up to ten o'clock now, the early morning rush hour appears to be easing off. Most of the main routes are moving well and there doesn't appear to be many problems.
Bobby	And what's the situation on the coast Frances?
Frances	A different story altogether there Bobby. At Ferryton there are traffic cues almost going back to the motorway. The car parks are filling up and there are dozens of coaches unloading on the sea front. Well, that's all from me Bobby. See you tomorrow.
Bobby	Bye, Frances. Well, there she goes. And wouldn't you just like to be the early worm picked up by our very own sultry whirlybird – Frances Fairweather?
Mr Scream	Aaaaaaghhh!
Bobby	No, no back in your cage Mr Scream. Well that's almost all from me this morning. Just to remind you that I will be 'doing a gig' down at 'Hollywood Nights' fun pub and disco in Ferryton tonight, so I look forward to seeing all you 'ravers' down there later. Stay tuned for more music after the news here on …
Jingle	West, West, West Coast Radio.
Bobby	You have been listening to 'Brews Up' sponsored this morning by Witherbrains West Country cider. And I'll leave you with a track for all those folks getting off the coaches down on Ferryton seafront right now – the Bluebells with 'Young at Heart'.

Music 'Young at Heart'. Lights up on Mavis, Dot and Betty who are getting off a coach.

Mavis	(*striding boldly out*) Well, here we are then ladies. Back at Ferryton-on-Sea for the twenty fifth year in a row. Once more we arrive to commemorate the sad event that drew the three of us even more closely together than before. And what more depressing place could we find than this?
Betty	(*stuck behind Dot and calling for help*) Mavis!
Mavis	(*oblivious to the problem*) Just look at it. Each year it gets worse. I remember when this was such a nice, quiet town.
Betty	What's the matter Dot?
Dot	I can't get off the bus!
Mavis	And what's it turned into? All these flashing lights and arcade things. What these young people need is more fresh air. Just look at them. All white and pale. Look like they live under stones. Dress like it most of them too.
Betty	(*loudly*) Mavis!
Mavis	For goodness sake you two. What are you doing? You're holding everyone up.
Betty	It's Dot. She can't get off the bus.
Mavis	Why ever not. Are you not well Dorothy dear?
Dot	It's those doors.
Betty	What about the doors?
Dot	They're going to close on me. I know it. And then I'll get stuck.
Mavis	Dorothy, the doors will not close on you, the coach driver is in full control of them.
Betty	She had a bad experience at Tesco's. Those revolving doors? Kept on going round and round and when she did try to get out she got caught in between them. She found it very distressing.
Dot	Look at him. He's not wearing a uniform. How do we know he is the bus driver?

Mavis	Dorothy, that young man may not be as upstanding as Mr Jones on the old number 42 who was a true gentleman in every sense of the word, but I do not believe he means to trap you in the doors of his coach. Do you dear? . . . No, there you see?
Betty	I think it's those horror videos her grandson brings round to hers to watch. I think they're having an effect on her.
Dot	I didn't want to come here anyroad. I wanted to go to Alton Towers.
Mavis	We'll take you on the pier dear. That's just like Alton Towers. You'll like that.
Dot	He wants his revenge you see.
Betty	Oh she's on about her Harold again. She's been like this all week.
Mavis	Dorothy. Get off the bus this instant and stop this nonsense.
Dot	You're a bully you are.
Mavis	Now, Dorothy.
Dot	Alright, alright. Watch him though. He could have my head off.

She steals herself and jumps past the doors. They finally manage to get off.

Betty	Thank goodness for that. I could see us being stuck there all day.
Mavis	Well I think we should go to the Winter Gardens for a cup of tea don't you?
Betty	That sounds just the ticket.
Dot	We always do the same thing. I want to do something different.
Mavis	Dorothy, not having to do anything different is one of the privileges of being our age.
Dot	I don't care. What's that over there? Let's do that instead.
Betty	What – that! We couldn't do that. It's one of those whatjer callits.

Mavis	A bouncy castle I think they're called. And most unsuitable for you Dorothy.
Betty	Yes, come on Dot. We don't want to have to call the ambulance again do we. Not after that time at Hampton Court Maze.
Dot	Looks like fun.
Mavis	Looks like a recipe for disaster to me. No, a brisk walk along the prom and a cup of tea before a fish and chip lunch as usual. Then down to the quay side to pay our respects to our tragically departed husbands, and then on to the afternoon sequence dance.
Betty	Come on then Dot.
Dot	She's a bully that one. Always has her own way. What's that girl doing over there with that suitcase and that knapsack?
Mavis	Well she's not out to get you that's for certain. Now come on.
Dot	She looks sad and lonely.
Mavis	All young people look like that nowadays. It's the air. Now come on.

The three old ladies shuffle off. A spotlight comes up on Jackie

Jackie	He said it would be safer if we travelled separately. Less chance of us being traced. I told him no-one would come after us but he insisted.
	It was difficult at the bus station. Getting on that bus made it all seem so final – so certain. I got off and I went to phone mum. I just wanted to hear her voice again. But then I thought that if I did, I wouldn't have the nerve to leave anymore. So I put the phone back on the hook and got on the bus.
	When I told Dave, he was so calm and so strong. He didn't say much really but I could just tell that he would think of something. I love him so much. I wish he could have met me at the station. Still, it will be really romantic to meet him on the end of the pier.

I love it here – where we met. There's an excitement about it. The sounds the lights – maybe that was something to do with why I let him. But I wanted to and he said everything would be alright. And it will be.

He said it's easy to get work at the seaside. Loads of places to live as well. This would be a good place to start a family – by the sea. Those people over there getting out of the car. They look like a nice family, they're having fun. Perhaps that'll be me and Dave someday. Perhaps.

She turns and goes to 'meet' him. As she does so the Brights briskly arrive

Ray	Well here we are everybody.
Hope	Wizard.
Sonny	Super.
Rosy	Lovely.
Ray	I must say, it's jolly convenient to be able to park straight on the beach like this.
Rosy	Isn't it just. I can leave the lunch safely in the car and come back to get it later.
Hope	Won't it get awfully hot though Mummy.
Sonny	Warm sandwiches!
Hope & Sonny	Yeuch!
Rosy	You're forgetting the cool bag that Daddy bought last year.
Ray	Did you bring it?
Rosy	I certainly did. So that means a wonderful cool and fresh meal for us.
Hope & Sonny	Hoorah!
Ray	All these new inventions are so exciting aren't they?
Rosy	What will they think of next?

Hope	Gosh, isn't it smashing here.
Sonny	Let's go and explore.
Ray	First you must help mother and I to set up our 'camp'.
Rosy	Yes, we have all the chairs and the blankets and the windbreaker to set up.
Sonny	Of course we'll help you Mummy. I'm sorry. It's just that it's all so thrilling and I forgot myself for a moment.
Ray	That's alright Sonny. We know you didn't mean to be so thoughtless.
Hope	Daddy, it's everso hot isn't it . . .
Ray	Yes . . .
Hope	And carrying all of those things will be hard work won't it . . .
Ray	Yes . . .
Hope	And we'll get all sweaty won't we . . .
Ray	Yes . . .
Hope	So if we could have something cold now . . .
Rosy	I think that Hope is hinting at something don't you Daddy?
Ray	I think she is.
Sonny	(*he has no idea*) What? What?
Ray	Oh very well. You can both have ice creams.
Hope & **Sonny**	Hoorah!
Sonny	Do you know to make ice cream?
Hope	No. How?
Sonny	An ice cube down my back – that makes **I . . . scream!**
Rosy	I say, Sonny's made a joke!

They all laugh loudly

Ray	Jolly witty Sonny.

Sonny	Thank you Daddy.
Ray	Well here's some money. You can go to the van over there on the prom.
Hope	You mean we can buy our own!
Ray	Well you are both getting older now and you must learn to accept these responsibilities.
Hope & **Sonny**	Wow!
Rosy	Now off you go but be careful.
Hope	We will be, Mummy. Look it's real money. Not toy money – real money!

Hope and Sonny go off clearly awed by their new level of responsibility.

Ray	What a wonderful pair of children we have dear.
Rosy	And what a worry they are.
Ray	I know. Just think. This time next year we'll be waiting for their GCSE results.
Rosy	Dear me. They grow up fast don't they.

Lights down. Music – 'Albatross'. Brights exeunt and scene switches to the chorus

Chorus	As the heat haze shimmers from the pavements,
	Suntan lotion is stroked on pallid skins.
	Ice-cold drinks are in hot demand and
	Ice creams run in white veins along writhing wrists.
	Castles sprouting paper flags, erupt from the sand
	As parents are lost beneath the beach.
	From every wall and bus-shelter,
	Fish and chips are devoured with pilgrim-like fervour
	And wheeling in the air, the gulls swoop on every
	uneaten morsel.

Chorus exits as Gull 1 circles the stage and spies a tasty morsel

Gull 1	Blimey, look at that. Left half his fish. I'm having that.
Gull 2	*(swooping in to land)* What you got there?
Gull 1	Fish – what's it look like?
Gull 2	Give us it.

Gull 1	Sod off. Get yer own.
Gull 2	No, I want that one.
Gull 1	It's mine.
Gull 2	Oh yeah?
Gull 1	Yeah?
Gull 2	Yeah!
Gull 1	I'll have you pal.
Gull 2	Oh yeah?
Gull 1	Come on then.

Gull 3 lands and starts to take the fish

Gull 1	(noticing Gull 3) Oi! What you think you're doin'?
Gull 3	Eatin' this fish.
Gull 2	That's mine
Gull 3	Got your name on it has it?
Gull 1	It's not 'is – it's mine.
Gull 3	Well I'm eatin' it.
Gull 2	No you ain't.
Gull 3	Who says?
Gull 1	I do.
Gull 3	I'll have the pair of yer.
Gull 2	Oh yeah?
Gull 3	Easy mate, no problem.
Gull 1	We'll see about that pal.
Gull 3	Yeah?
Gull 2	Stitch this pal.
Gull 3	Is that your best shot? I'll have you.
Gull 1	Yeah?
Gull 2	Come on then.

Gull 4 arrives and starts on the fish

Gull 3	(noticing Gull 4) What the hell you doin'?

Gull 4	Eatin' this fish.
Gull 2	No you ain't.
Gull 4	Well I'm not riding a bike am I.
Gull 1	That's my fish.
Gull 2	I'm gonna sort you out.
Gull 1	You and whose . . .
Gull 4	(spying an approaching car) Car! Car!

The Gulls fly off and circle for a few moments. Then they fly back

Gull 1	I'm telling you it's mine.
Gull 4	Get lost.
Gull 3	You too pal.
Gull 2	Touch it and I'll peck your eye out.
Gull 1	Go sit on a lamppost beaky.
Gull 2	Oo you callin' beaky – string legs.
Gull 3	Don't push me.
Gull 4	What you gonna do about it?
Gull 2	Just you wait.
Gull 1	Yeah?
Gull 3	Yeah.
Gull 2	Yeah?
Gull 4	Yeah.

Pause. The gulls 'transform' into the chorus

Chorus	And it goes on
	And on
	And on
	And on and on the sun beats down
	While the temperatures rise
	The pavements are scorching
	Everyone fries.
	And about to arrive now
	Almost straight from their beds
	Are the guys – the lads

Still nursing thick heads.

The scene switches as 'the boys' dash on to the stage area.

Brian	Bri!
Kevin	Kev!
Jason	Jayce!
Darren	And Daza!
Brian	We are . . .
All	The Boys!

Music. 'The Boys are Back in Town'. Music fades

Kevin	(*peering at the beach*) Look at it. The beach is packed.
Jason	Swarming with talent.
Brian	Yeah.
Kevin	This is the life mate.
Darren	That sun's a bit bright.
Brian	Don't complain about it.
Jason	Should get yourself a pair of Raybans like mine.
Darren	I'm not mug enough to spend ninety quid on a pair of sunglasses am I.
Jason	Your problem is you've got no style.
Darren	But I've got ninety quid more than you.
Jason	When the girls see these it sends the message – sophistication.
Darren	A pity the rest of you sends the message – Dickhead!
Kevin	Are we gonna stand here talkin' all day or what?
Brian	Yeah come on.
Kevin	We've got to get exactly the right spot. Not too far from the prom so we can make an impression on the passing talent.
Brian	A bit of space so we can attract some in.
Jason	Near enough to some lookers so we can cop an eyeful.

Darren	And well away from the toddlers and the grannies.
Brian	Too right.
Kevin	How about over there by those two?
Jason	The redhead's all right. What's 'er mate like though.
Brian	Hey, she's sittin' up

They all look intensely — they are disappointed by what they see

All	(*shaking their heads*) Nah.
Darren	Hey look at those four just arriving.
Kevin	All right.
Brian	Tasty.
Jason	Smart.
Kevin	Let's watch and see where they go.

Music 'Girls just Wanna have Fun'. *Lads freeze and the scene switches to the four girls arriving.*

Cheryl	Look at the place. It's heaving.
Tina	Like you last night you mean?
Cheryl	Ha ha.
Mandy	It's so hot. Have to be careful not to burn.
Karen	Should be like me. I had eight sessions on the sun bed down the health club before I came away.
Cheryl	Wondered how you had a tan like that with the weather we've had.
Tina	Thought that was bad for you?
Karen	Depends what you want. A tan makes me feel good and look good. And fellers notice a girl with a tan.
Tina	Judging by most of the blokes I've seen, I'm glad I'm brilliant white then.
Mandy	I tried one of those instant tans once — came out bright orange. I felt like a Belisha beacon!
Cheryl	Let's find somewhere to sit down.
Karen	Yeah, we've got to get a decent spot.

Tina	Most of the good places have gone.
Mandy	What about over there. It's quite a big space.
Cheryl	Yeah, that'll do.
Mandy	Hang on those blokes are taking it.
Cheryl	Typical!
Karen	What are they like? I haven't put my contact lenses in yet.
Mandy	Well, they're not exactly the Chippendales.
Cheryl	Thank god for that.
Karen	Ooh, I like some muscle me
Tina	And we all know which one! There's still enough space next to them for us.
Karen	What do you reckon then?
Cheryl	Can't see anywhere else round here.
Karen	Come on then. No sense in wasting my sun tan is there?

Lights down on the girls. Up on the lads

Jason	You sure this will work?
Kevin	Absolutely. Look around. This is the last bit of space. If we get set up here, carefully leaving just enough room over there ... they're bound to take it.
Brian	You reckon?
Kevin	Trust me. You're talkin' to a master of his craft here mate.
Darren	Bet it doesn't work.
Kevin	How much?
Darren	A fiver.
Kevin	You're on pal.

They shake hands

Brian	Come on let's get sorted.
Jason	Yeah, give us a hand with these towels Daz.

Darren	Alright.
Kevin	Hey, over here a bit more. If it's too cramped they won't fancy it.
Darren	There's no chance.
Kevin	Just you wait sunshine.
Brian	Anybody want some breakfast?
Jason	Yeah.
Darren	Sling us one.
Kevin	Don't mind if I do squire.

They each catch a ring pull can from Brian. They open the cans, simultaneously, take three enormous gulps, exhale loudly, wipe their mouths with the backs of their hands, and burp.

All	That's better.
Brian	Eh, Kev. Those birds are headin' this way.
Kevin	Let's make 'em feel welcome then! Down to the basics.
Jason	Best baggy T-shirt – off in a flash.
All	Whoosh (*they remove their T-shirts*).
Darren	Down to designer deep cut vests.
Brian	Reebok trainers flicked off with expertise.
All	Whoosh (*one shoe is flicked off and caught*).
All	Whoosh (*the other shoe follows*).
Kevin	With well oiled precision, tracksuit bottoms are dropped.
All	Whoosh (*they remove their tracksuit bottoms*).
Jason	Revealing baggy swim shorts of every shade and hue.
Brian	Swimming trunks?
All	No way!
Darren	And now the *piece de resistance*.
Kevin	The *coup de grace*.
Brian	In best male model tradition.
Jason	We dispense with the vests.

Music. 'I'm Too Sexy'. In a 'Full Monty' type routine they slowly wriggle out of their vests.

Darren   I don't believe it – they're bought it.

The girls enter the pool of light.

Brian   (*to audience*) So straight away it's into the pose.

They go into male model/hunk type poses which they hold during the next scene. We switch to the girls.

Mandy   What do you reckon then?

Karen   The one in the middle. He's cute.

Tina   You think so! Looks like a prat to me.

Cheryl   Come on. Let's get settled. I want to have a nice long sleep.

Mandy   Watch you don't burn.

Cheryl   I'll be fine.

Tina   (*to audience*) And in the blink of an eye, the sundress is gone.

All   Swish (*shoulder strap*) Swish (*shoulder strap*) Swoosh (*dress falls to floor*)

Mandy   But there's no embarrassment, we've our swimsuits on!

Cheryl   Simple one piece, plain but practical. Had it since school.

Tina   Gold micro two piece – like three hankies tied up with string.

Mandy   Black wet look one piece, sophisticated and cool.

Karen   In luminous green, low, low cut back, high, high cut thighs. I look at the lads (*she does so*) and they're all eyes.

Lights up on lads. Looking at Karen

Lads   Bloody hell!

Tina   To attract such attention our swimsuits we chose.

Cheryl   And now that we've got it, it's into our pose.

Pause. The girls pose in female model type poses.

Mandy   Impression created, and glances exchanged.

The lads and the girls exchange simultaneous glances.

Brian   Time for sunbathing, so on with the shades.

Lads and girls all put on sunglasses. They settle down to sunbathe.

Chorus   So this is the beach in early afternoon

                   In sweltering heat we almost swoon.

                   Inhibitions melt in response to temptation

                   Palms are sweating in anticipation.

Everyone is on the beach. The focus is on the girls who are being closely watched by the nearby lads.

Karen   You're not serious.

Tina   Yeah. Why not?

Karen   Well just look around you.

Tina   Nobody will notice.

Mandy   You reckon if you take your top off on this beach
                   nobody will notice? You must have a screw loose.

Cheryl   Wouldn't catch me doing it.

Tina   Just 'cause you haven't got the bottle.

Karen   I did it last year, when I went to Ibiza. I didn't mind
                   there.

Tina   So why not here?

Karen   Well everyone does it abroad. This is Ferryton-on-Sea
                   for heaven's sake. I can't see any one else doin' it
                   round here – can you?

Tina   Only takes one to have the nerve.

Cheryl   You really fancy yourself you do.

Tina   At least I'm not ashamed of my body.

Mandy   Isn't it illegal.

Tina   No-one will even notice. Look at 'em all. And even if
                   they do, they won't make a fuss will they!

Cheryl	Hey Karen, you're always goin' on about your tan. Why don't you have a go?
Karen	It's her idea.
Cheryl	Chicken.
Karen	Look if she does it and it's alright then so will I.
Tina	Promise.
Karen	If you go first – yeah.
Tina	Right here we go then.

She begins to undo her top

Mandy	Hey, come on you two – you'll get us arrested.
Tina	There!

She removes her top and looks around

Tina	See no-one has even ...

For a moment nothing happens then suddenly everyone looks in her direction. All make remarks, point, stare etc. Tina reacts, lies down on her front and desperately tries to recover her top ...

Lads	Tits! Tits! Tits!
Tina	Shit!

Tina continues to cover her embarrassment and waves shyly at the boys.

Music. 'Guaglione'. **Movement sequence**. *During the music we see the beach fill up and folks indulge in beach activities, setting up 'camps', sunbathing, playing games, going for a paddle etc. all in time to the music. At the close all on stage freeze*

Chorus	As Ferryton basks in Mediterranean heat
	Families indulge in family fun
	Unaware of the terror they might meet
	In this halcyon scene of tranquillity and sun.
	For right under their noses, almost ready to begin
	Lurks a dark and sinister temple to sin.
	Which enshrines such abominable evils as,
	Child abuse!
	Violence and murder!
	Disregard for law and order!
	Cruelty to animals!

And cannibalism!
For with a mighty cry of
'That's the way to do it'
Mr Punch comes to town.
Around the canvas booth hoards of children gather.

All become young children moving to see the Punch and Judy show

All   We want Mr Punch, we want Mr Punch!

Chorus   But today will be different from the word go
                 For Roberta and Shirley – new age feminist
                 puppeteers – are presenting this show.

Roberta   Well it looks like we're about ready. There's quite a big
                 crowd gathered.

Shirley   Right, let's get on with it.

Roberta   Do you really think they will like it? I think most of
                 them are expecting a traditional Punch and Judy
                 Show.

Shirley   Well the sign's clear enough isn't it. 'Mr Punch – the
                 new age man!'

Roberta   I suppose so.

Shirley   Come on then. Let's influence some impressionable
                 minds and strike a blow for peace and radical
                 feminism. I'll get in the booth and you give the
                 announcement.

She 'enters the booth' and joins children watching the show

Roberta   Hello boys and girls!

All   Hello!

Roberta   Are you ready to see Mr Punch?

All   Yeah.

Roberta   You'll have to shout louder than that. I'll count to
                 three and then everyone shout, as loud as you can,
                 'Hello Mr Punch'.

                 One, two, three!

All   Hello Mr Punch!

Roberta exits and joins the crowd. Mr Punch jumps up from the stage

Punch	Hello Boys and Girls.
All	Hello Mr Punch.
Punch	Have you seen my wife, Judy?
All	No!
Punch	Well I wonder where she's got to?

Judy enters, behind Punch

All	She's behind you!
Punch	(turning the wrong way) Oh no she isn't.
All	The other way.
Punch	This way? (Turning the wrong way)
All	The **other** way!
Punch	This way?
All	No!
Punch	Well which way . . . Oh there she is. Hello Judy!
Judy	Hello Punch!

They embrace

Judy	Punch, now that my maternity leave is over I'm resuming my job as a lawyer.
Punch	But what about the baby.
Judy	I thought you could look after her.
Punch	Of course dear. Anything to help further your career prospects.
Judy	Here she is then, Bye.

Exit Judy. The baby starts to cry

Punch	Oh dear, what am I going to do?
Little boy	Throw it out the window.
Shirley	(off) Of course, he's not going to throw her out the window you vicious little brat.
Roberta	(off) Shirley!
Punch	I know I'll take her for a walk in the pram. I'm not

	embarrassed to be seen in public with my child. Here we go. (Exit)
Judy	(entering) Oh where's my baby, where's my baby?
Girl	They've gone for a walk.
Boy	This is boring.
Judy	I'll go to the park and see if I can find them. (Exit Judy)
Punch	(entering) Morning Mr Policeman, have you been cleared of those assault charges?
Policeman	I certainly have. And what about you Mr Punch? Do you still own the sausage factory?
Punch	Certainly not. I'm a vegetarian now! And despite much evidence to the contrary I still have faith in the essential honesty of most of the police force.
Policeman	Good day Mr Punch.

(Judy enters)

Punch	Look it's Judy. Hello Judy!
Judy	Hello Punch. Eeeeek! Look.
Punch	Don't worry dear. It's only an escaped crocodile.

The crocodile enters

Judy	Kill it. Kill it.
Punch	We can't do that – it's an endangered species. Let's phone the zoo so they can look after it.
Judy	Or we could ring the RSPCA?
Punch	What shall we do children? Shall we phone the zoo?

Pause

	Children?
Roberta	They've all gone.
Shirley	But we were just getting to the good bit where Mr Punch joins Greenpeace and saves the whole Eco system!
Roberta	I don't understand it!

Music. Scene switches to the chorus

Chorus	Afternoon at Ferryton and beached bodies bake.
	Girls getting tanned, boys on the make.
	But here, at last, finally arrived,
	After losing their way in the countryside
	Are Wayne and Sharron, almost within reach
	Of their day out on the beach.

The Killjoys enter and stand looking at their 'car' in disbelief.

Wayne	I don't believe this.
Sharron	Well don't look at me!
Wayne	It were your bloody idea weren't it.
Sharron	All I said was, it would have been nice to have parked closer to the pier. I didn't tell yer to just drive along the beach like this.
Carrie	If we hadn't got lost, we could have got in one of the nearer car parks.
Wayne	Alright, alright.
Carrie	It took us ages to get here.
Wayne	Give it a rest will yer.
Damien	Are we really stuck Dad?
Wayne	What does it look like?
Sharron	We've been trying to get out for five minutes. You can't get much more stuck than that.
Damien	Didn't you see the sign saying 'Danger, soft sand', Dad? Didn't yer?
Wayne	Course I didn't.
Damien	I did. I saw it. It said 'Danger soft sand' and I thought, 'If we go down here we're going to get stuck' and we did!
Sharron	Shurrup Damien. What do you want – a medal?
Carrie	Can I go to the arcades? They've got one of those 'Virtual Reality' games there.
Wayne	Isn't this real enough for yer?
Carrie	Look, I didn't want to come in the first place. I could

be at home but I'm stuck here with you lot and the car buried up to its axles in sand. This is not my idea of a great time. I'm going to the arcades.

She exits

Wayne	Carrie! Carrie get back 'ere!
Damien	Mum, what about me? Can I get a burger? I'm starvin'. Can I mum eh? Can I please?
Sharron	Oh go on then. 'Ere y'are.
Damien	Great.

She hands over some money and Damien exits

Wayne	He'll get that bloody mad cow disease the way he sticks back all those bloody burgers.
Sharron	I'd worry if I thought I'd notice any difference. What are we going to do?
Wayne	Well no sense in wasting the day. You take the stuff and get set up further along the beach and I'll get the car dug out.
Sharron	Shouldn't you ring for a tow truck or something?
Wayne	Can't soddin' afford it after that cream tea. £17.50. I couldn't believe that.
Sharron	You sure? I don't think you'll be able to just dig it out.
Wayne	Course I will. Look just leave it to me will ya?
Sharron	Suits me fine. (*She exits*)

Music plays – 'Ride on Time'. He looks out to sea and then looks again with a more anxious gaze. He screams in time to the screams in the music and gestures frantically out to sea. Lights fade. The scene switches to the Brights

Wayne	Peace at last. What a mess. Still, good job the tide's out eh.
Sonny	I say, Mother, Father we just saw something that was jolly amusing.
Hope	We did. It was killing.
Ray	Well don't keep us in suspense.
Rosy	Yes. Do tell.

Hope	We were just walking back along the beach after investigating the rock pools at the end of the bay.
Sonny	Which were simply thrilling. There were limpets, and sea weed and I found a crab but it was dead.
Rosy & Ray	Eeurgh!
Rosy	Oh dear, I hope you didn't touch it.
Sonny	Well actually we did. We dug it a little grave and buried it. We marked the spot with a paper union jack on a stick. Sorry Mother.
Ray	I think that under the circumstances you can be forgiven, don't you Mother?
Rosy	Just this once.
Sonny	Thanks Mummy.
Hope	Are you sure it was dead. I thought I saw it move.
Sonny	Course it was dead.
Hope	How do you know?
Sonny	Because I do.
Hope	Don't.
Sonny	Do!
Rosy	Children now don't be silly.
Ray	Yes tell us the rest of your interesting story.
Hope	We . . . ell, we saw that a car had got stuck on the beach.
Rosy	Oh dear. How unfortunate.
Hope	Mmm, yes. Definitely. But then came the funny part.
Sonny	The tide is coming in!
Hope	Oh I wanted to tell that bit.
Sonny	Sorry Sis. Forgive me?
Hope	I suppose so.
They hug	
Ray & Rosy	Aaah!

Ray	Well, I suppose it is rather amusing, still it is a little wicked to have fun at other people's misfortune.
Rosy	Should we offer to help?
Ray	Oh no dear. A person reckless enough to drive a car along a beach might be capable of anything.
Rosy	You're probably right. Best keep ourselves to ourselves.
Ray	And now children I have a special treat!
Sonny	Gosh. What is it Daddy?
Rosy	Well, while you were away daddy set up his new camera on a . . . what was it dear?
Ray	A tripod.
Hope	Golly.
Rosy	And that means that we can have a photograph with us all in it to commemorate our wonderful day at the seaside.
Hope	But how Daddy?
Ray	My new camera has a special timer on it which will take the photograph for us.
Hope	Can I do it Daddy? Please, please please!
Ray	Very well. When we are in position just press this button and run back to us.
Hope	Gosh thanks Father!
Rosy	Right, are we all ready? I've left a space for you next to me Hope.
Hope	Thanks Mummy. Right, say 'cheese'.
All	Cheese!
Hope	Daddy, I don't think it's going!
Ray	It is. I can see the little red light flashing.
Sonny	Come on Hope. Run.
Hope	Are you sure?
There is a flash	
Hope	Oh dear.

Rosy	Too late.
Sonny	Girls!
Hope	Oh dear, I am hopeless or at least the photograph will be – **hope** – **less**!
Ray	I say, Hope has made a joke!

They all laugh hysterically. There is a flash and they all freeze. Lights out

Chorus	Now on the beach in mid afternoon
	In dream laden haze the day slips by
	When into the drowsy numbness seeps
	A distant rhythmic flat four thud.
	The sunbathers stir to momentary attention
	As carried on a sound wave, coming their way
	The west coast sound of the Beach Boys singing,
	'Fun, fun, fun' and 'Surfin USA'.

We hear a distant 'Surfin USA'

Chorus	Yes the surfers are in town!
	Slowly cruising along the prom in their
	Volkswagen Beetle Cabriolet
	Engine race tuned at Arnie's
	Twin exhausts, accessories by Kamei
	In deep midnight blue.
	Lacquered with mother of pearl flecks
	An airbrushed Hawaiian wave crashes
	Along the side – this is a car to respect!
	They pull into a parking space
	And leap out over the side
	Grab their surfboards and hit the sand
	They've got to catch the tide.

The surfers run into centre stage and strike suitably heroic positions.

Mat	Hi, I'm Matt
Fraser	I'm Fraser.
Clive	And I'm Clive.
All	We're here on a mission,
	We're surfin kinda guys.

They strike a pose

Matt	We've conquered every beach on the west coast.
Fraser	Except one – Ferryton-on-Sea.
Clive	But today is the day.
Fraser	Today **is** the day.
Matt	We've calculated the tide times and strengths.
Clive	Studied weather reports.
Fraser	Examined the currents and coastline.
Matt	Watched the barometer like hawks.
Clive	This time the signs are right.
Fraser	At precisely 2.45 there will be waves.
Matt	Time?
Fraser	2.43.
Clive	The sea is calm, totally flat.
Matt	Just wait, we'll get the waves. I can feel them.

They freeze for a moment

Clive	Nothing.
Fraser	Barely a ripple.
Matt	Wait!
Clive	And right at that moment, a slight change in the current.
Fraser	A barely perceptible on shore breeze.
Clive	And there, glimmering, glinting in the sun, is . . .
All	The Wave!
Fraser	Totally awesome.
Matt	Most excellent.
Clive	Bodacious in the extreme!
Matt	Come on guys!

They quickly strip to their wet suits

Fraser	Grab the boards.

Clive	Polished and waxed to perfection.
Matt	Fins as sharp as razors.
Fraser	Fluorescent and neon works of art with credentials to match.
Matt	Fat Willy's Surf Shack (*Slapping a sticker on the board*) — bosh.
Clive	Fat Willy's Surf Shack — bosh.
Fraser	Fat Willy's Surf Shack — bosh, bosh, bosh.
Matt	And its into the waves!

They charge forward. As they enter the water they scream.

Fraser	It's freezin'!
Clive	It's cold!
Matt	It's ice!

They all look down and examine themselves.

All	Small Willy's — Surf Shock!

Lights out. Surfers exit. Lights up on Chorus

Chorus	And so they plunge through the breakers
	Further and further out they go.
	Fascinated onlookers peer from the beach
	To see them do battle with their foe!
	They seem, as they turn towards the shore,
	Like knights of bygone days
	Fighting the dancing silver crests
	They're up, they're riding the waves!

Music: 'Wipe out' by the Surfaris. The surfers enter. They are 'surfing' standing up in shopping trolleys, pushed around the stage by other members of the cast. They perform a 'surfing' routine with elaborate turns and spins in time to the music. Those pushing the trolleys join in with 60's 'Go Go' style dancing. As the routine ends the music fades . . .

Matt	We've done it guys!
Clive	Every beach in the West.
Fraser	Totally triumphant!
Clive	Hey man, I don't believe it. There's another guy surfing!

Fraser	You can't be serious!
Clive	Look, over there. He's even jumping and waving about!
Matt	Neat tricks but say, that's not a surfboard he's on.
Clive	You're right. It looks more like . . .
Fraser	The roof of a car!
All	Cool!
Matt	Hey guys, I hate to dampen your enthusiasm but . . .
Clive	But what?
Matt	A pipeline! A tube!
Fraser	Hey Matt, these waves are OK but a pipeline – no way.
Matt	Way! But I'm not talkin' surf man, I'm talkin' sewage outfall.
Clive	Where?
Matt	There.
Fraser	Oh no!
Matt	Most non-sanitary!
Clive	Excremental in the extreme!
All	Wipe out!

As they 'fall' the lights go out. Spotlight up on the Chorus

Chorus	The bedraggled trio struggle ashore,
	Their objective gained but at some cost.
	They've vanquished every beach in the West
	But their poise, image and cool, they've lost.
	At least now they know that at Ferryton,
	As a result of their devotions,
	The surfing may not be great,
	But they can, go through the motions.

Lights out. Surfers exit under cover of music. The scene switches to the three donkeys.

Stan	By heck, I didn't think much of the Punch and Judy show did you Norbert?
Norbert	It was a bit rum Stan, I'll give thee that.

Eric	Well what happened to the bit where they throw the baby about?
Norbert	Dunno Eric. It's the sausage machine that I like best. Always a source of grim satisfaction that.
Stan	I'll tell thee something else.
Eric	Go on then Stan.
Stan	At least we usually get a rest while the show's on. Not today though.
Norbert	No, they were all over us. (*Kicking out*) Get away there!
Eric	It's hard work in all this heat.
Norbert	What's the current score then Eric?
Eric	You've got four, I've got four an all and Stan's got six.
Norbert	Stroke of genius going for that low beam under the pier Stan. I'll give thee that.
Stan	Not only unsaddled but concussed as well.

They all laugh in their braying fashion.

Eric	Old Dawson didn't look too pleased did he?
Stan	'Fraid not. Heard him saying I was going to have to be hitched up to Thunderbird One if I did it again.
Norbert	That little kid is still at it!
Eric	What swingin' on yer tail?
Norbert	Right enough. And just look at his mother. Don't care about me just wants it on video. It's right painful.
Stan	Hey Norbert. You could catch that kid a good one now.
Norbert	Is he in position?
Eric	Bit to your left. Steady. That'll do.
Norbert	Right. Bombs away.

Norbert grimaces with the effort.

Stan	A beauty.
Eric	Right on top of his head.
Norbert	Whiffy an all!

They laugh again

Norbert   What's his mother doin'?

Stan   That's the funny thing. She's standing there laughin' and talkin' about *You've been Framed!*

Eric   And she's still got the video running. As long as I live I will never understand human beings.

Norbert   Seems to have taken the pleasure out of it somehow.

Stan   That's life for yer Norbert.

Norbert   Happen you're right there Stan. Happen you're right.

Eric   Hey up Stan, over on the old quay side. See who I see?

Stan   I do Eric. It's those old dears again. Same place, same day every year without fail. How long have they been comin' here?

Norbert   Oooh. Can't be sure but I tell thee what . . . it must be donkey's years!

They do their braying laugh again. Music 'Justified and Ancient' Light comes up on Mavis, Betty and Dot.

Mavis   Well here we are ladies. Once more we gather to pay our loving respects. Have you got the wreath there Betty?

Betty   I have Mavis. I asked old Mrs Hagan from the WI to make it up especially for us. She's very good at the floral tributes is Agnes.

Mavis   And what is the charge for her endeavours?

Betty   Just five pounds. She managed to find some good left overs when she was cleaning through the church last Sunday.

Dot   It's a waste just throwing all these nice flowers over this wall. Look much nicer on my sideboard at home.

Mavis   That's as may be Doris but it would hardly be a tribute to our departed husbands to be commemorated in your rear parlour would it.

Dot   It's all a bit spooky if you ask me. I can feel 'em all watchin' us. Like that Tony Blair thing.

Mavis	The Prime Minister Dot?
Betty	It's all right – she's talking about a film she's seen. Here's the card Mavis. 'In loving memory of Arthur, Sidney and Harold who vanished beneath these waters in 1968.'
Mavis	Succinct and to the point Betty. Well done.
Dot	(*looking down*) The sea's all brown and mucky!
Betty	It's always like that Dot.
Dot	Not like sea at all really.
Mavis	Are we ready ladies?
Betty	Certainly Mavis.
Dot	I want an ice cream. One of those ones with a flake in it.

The other two look at her.

Dot	But I suppose it can wait.
Mavis	Right. Once again we gather to remember how twenty-five years ago to this very day, our husbands were taken from us. How their hired fishing boat sank beneath the waves and all three of them, being non-swimmers and not having the benefit of life-jackets, perished in these waters.
	We give thanks for the salesman who had persuaded us to take out such large life insurance policies which have enabled us to live so comfortably since the tragedy. And despite the fact that Arthur, Sidney and Harold were three of the biggest drunken, wife-beating bastards the sun has ever shed it's light on, we hope that they can find it in their hearts to forgive us.
Betty	It's a good job you remembered to throw out those life-jackets, Mavis.
Mavis	But it was Dorothy's idea of replacing the bung in the bottom of the boat with a slab of soap that was the true stroke of genius.
Dot	Harold never washed. Stank to high heaven he did. Wouldn't have recognised soap if he had eaten it.
Mavis	Right, chuck the wreath over Betty.

Betty	Here we go then.

She throws the wreath over the side. They all watch it go.

Dot	You don't think he's going to reach up and grab it do you?
Betty	You're going to have to stop watching those videos Dot. Mavis, how many more years are we going to have to come and do this?
Mavis	For the rest of our lives Betty. To be on the safe side. That Mrs Bassett from number thirty-two has always had her suspicions.
Betty	It's a small price to pay I suppose.
Dot	But I want to go to Disneyland next year.
Mavis	Then we will go in the Spring. We have to come here to maintain our alibi.
Dot	Can I have an ice cream now then?
Betty	I suppose so Dot.
Dot	And a trip on the pier?
Mavis	Very well Dorothy – after the sequence dance at the Winter Gardens.
Dot	Come on then. I'm going to have some strawberry sauce as well.

She goes

Mavis	Do you have the wet wipes Betty?
Betty	I do.
Mavis	For I think that we shall have need of them. Come along.

They exit

Chorus	As the day slips slowly away The beach loses its attraction And red-shouldered tourists look to the pier In search of further distraction.

The scene switches to the Brights on the pier. Sonny and Hope are looking through a telescope.

Sonny	Come on Sis. It's my turn now.
Hope	No it isn't, you had much longer than me.
Sonny	But I want to look at the donkeys chasing after those screaming children.
Hope	Well you'll have to wait won't you. I'm still looking at the funny old lady on the bouncy castle!
Sonny	Oh please – just a quick look.
Hope	No – it's not your go. Now . . .
Sonny	Click!
Hope	Oh dear the times run out.
Ray	Well, let that be a lesson to you.
Rosy	Yes, see all the problems that arguing can cause.
Hope	Gosh mummy – you're right. Neither of us benefited from our dispute.
Sonny	We will certainly learn from our mistake won't we Hope?
Hope	We will Sonny – sorry.
Sonny	I'm sorry too sis.
Ray	Well what a wonderful day it has been.
Rosy	A wonderful day.
Hope & Sonny	Mmmmmm.
Rosy	But all good things have to come to an end.
Ray	I'm afraid they must.
Hope & Sonny	Ooow!
Hope	It was a lovely walk out along this pier.
Sonny	Thrilling.
Rosy	A fitting conclusion to our day's adventure.
Ray	But the excitement's not quite over yet. I have decided that rather than walk all the way back along the pier – which is a jolly long way.

Hope & Sonny	Mmmm.
Ray	We shall take the motorised, miniature pier train back to the promenade.
Hope & Sonny	Yippee!
Rosy	What a super treat.
Sonny	I say Mummy. Nobody has made a joke.
Rosy	We haven't have we!

They all laugh loudly

Sonny	Are you sure we can't have a quick look in the funfair at the end of the pier before we go Father?
Ray	I'm afraid not Sonny. We wouldn't want you mixing with the type of person who frequents such places.
Hope	And what sort of person is that, Father?

The scene quickly switches to the Killjoys.

Sharron	Oh come on Wayne. We'll miss the bus.
Wayne	I'm not leavin' until I've won something. This has been the most expensive day of my soddin life and I'm gonna get something out of it.
Carrie	I've never been so embarrassed as when those lifeguards rescued you.
Wayne	Alright.
Damien	Mum, my head still hurts!
Sharron	I told you not to go on those donkeys didn't I. You're too big.
Damien	It's not my fault. It threw me off. Vicious thing, should be locked up.
Carrie	A vicious donkey? You're pathetic you are.
Damien	What's gonna happen to the car now they've towed it out of the sea Dad?
Wayne	Scrap heap – it'd cost too much to repair with all that water in it.

Damien	We gonna get a new car then?
Sharron	It'll be all our savings gone.
Wayne	Nothing else we can do is there.
Carrie	Come on let's go.
Damien	I'm hungry.
Wayne	Just one more shot. If I can hit another ping-pong ball I'll win a prize.
Sharron	You said that ten minutes ago!
Wayne	Shhh.
Carrie	Hurry up.
All	Bang!
Carrie	I don't believe it!
Wayne	Yes! At last something on this bloody rotten day has gone right. I've won. I've won. I've won! (*He raises his arms in triumph*)
Sharron	And here's yer prize.
Wayne	(*taking it*) An inflatable banana! What the hell use is an inflatable banana?
Sharron	About as much use as you. Now come on kids lets get to that station.
Carrie	'Bout time!
Damien	Can I get some fish and chips on the way?

They all exit, leaving Wayne on his own. He looks at the banana.

Wayne	Well at least its better than nothing.

There is a bang and the sound of the banana deflating.

Wayne	Shit! What a day. What a bloody day!

He stands dejectedly looking down at the burst banana. Sharron re-enters

Sharron	Oh come on Wayne. What's happened to your banana?
Wayne	It's a bit limp!

They look at each other for a moment then burst into laughter!

Sharron	Well that's not like you Wayne! (*They laugh*) Come here. (*She hugs him*)
Wayne	(*embarrassed*) I was just trying to have a nice family day out!
Sharron	And I love you for tryin'.
Wayne	Carrie hates me.
Sharron	She's 18 – she's supposed to. It'll be all right when she goes up to that university in Oxford.
Wayne	I'm dead proud of her you know.
Sharron	I know. Come on

They begin to exit. Wayne puts his arm round Sharron and then tickles her playfully

Sharron	Wayne, none of that . . . Wayne!

They laugh and Wayne chases Sharron off. Lights down. Lights up on chorus

Chorus	Now Ferryton, a transformation undergoes For as the sun tumbles slowly in the west All the beach takes on its golden glow While the sea becomes a strip of amber fire Along the sea front the illuminations Like strings of glowing beats ignite. And the pier, an electric green strip, Divides the bay in two, like day from night. The night sneaks in and the middle- and old-aged depart. Now the prom belongs to the young. Bars and pubs teem with life. Danger and excitement mingle on this hot summer night! Yet still, at the pier's end, a young girl's vigil goes on.

(Jackie grows more and more desperate through this speech. By the end she is only barely in control of herself.)

Jackie	How much longer is he going to be? It's been so long. What if something has happened to him? What if he's been in an accident? How could they tell me? I would just be left here.

It's the not knowing that is the worst part. If only I knew what was happening. Then at least I could do something. What am I going to **do**? Where is he? Why isn't he here? It can't be his fault. I wouldn't leave me this long if he could help it.

When he comes everything will be alright. It will. And we can get a flat and everything will be fine and I won't have to worry anymore. I can't imagine being without him – I just can't. (*Pause*)

Maybe . . . maybe I was wrong. I was sure he said the pier. Meet on the pier where we met. Where we met? Perhaps he meant where we did it. The park along the cliff top, in those bushes. That must be it. He meant there – not here. He's probably been there all day waiting, blaming me. That's where he'll be. I know it. I know it.

She exits running. Blackout

Music: 'You Took the Words Right out of my Mouth'. *Lights up shortly after music begins*

Chorus   With a sound like an approaching earthquake – the boy racers arrive.
In red XR3's, black GTi's, they cruise the prom.
Windows wound down and cool shades on.
Car's reduced to hi-fi speakers – the volume set to overload.
The sound of The Fujees, De La Soul and Eminem sweeps the seafront.
All reduced, to knee twitching, spine shivering bass lines.
Three circuits round, bouncing the sleeping policemen with glee, then it's time to park and chat.
They pull up next to each other, a postcards width apart.
What's the point in having a car if you have to get out to talk?

Racer 1   (*they shout throughout*) Alright!

Racer 2   Alright. How yer doin'?

Racer 1   New system fitted. It's blindin'!

Racer 2   Oh yeah!

Racer 1   Four hundred watts into eight sub woofers,
interlinked into a 12″ Infinity base tube. Two four
inch metal tweeters in sound damped enclosures.
Dolby surround sound, solid core cabling, eighteen
channel graphic equaliser, auto-change head unit and
auto-reverse cassette deck. The volume control is
marked on the Richter scale and on four it gives you
nose bleeds.

Racer 2   Tidy! Susan not with you tonight?

Racer 1   Nah! No room left for her is there.

Chorus   And as more and more cars roll up, the police pass
but turn a blind eye.
A white Escort van screeches to a halt and the rear
doors are flung open wide.
Three feet high speakers hit the pavement and at full-
blast a mini rave begins.

*Music: 'Get Ready for This!' Strobe lights. Suddenly we are plunged into a rave, and
all dance manically only to suddenly stop moments later.*

Until at ten, it's time to join the queue outside
'Hollywood Nights.'
Half-price before eleven but for girls at any time it's
free.
Strictly neat dress – it's the best place in town.
With the toughest bouncers and a rigid admission
policy.

Scene switches to Psycho (the bouncer) outside the club. Some girls go past

Psycho   Evenin' girls. Watch yourselves tonight.

Girls go past

Psycho   Evenin' ladies. Mind yourselves tonight.

They giggle and go past

Psycho   Name's Perce, but the punters call me Psycho. Though never to me face, cause I'd deck 'em. Six feet four, solid muscle. Shaved head, totally smooth, except for me pony tail at the back – which is the source of my power. Look as hard as granite but I'm harder. Get the appearance right – you don't get so many problems. People look at me and think about hospital. Look too long and they go there. (*Laughs a ghoulish laugh*) Punters call me a bouncer – but I'm not. I'm a perimeter receptionist. Service with a smile. (*Almost painfully forces a ghoulish smile*) I still live with me mum but there's nothing wrong with that – is there!

Homerun (a smaller bouncer) enters

Homerun	Alright Perce.
Psycho	Alright Charlie.
Homerun	Charlie to me mates but me nickname's Homerun. I don't mind. Good to have a nickname. Me an Perce have been on the door at Hollywood Nights for three years now. We're a team. Some bloke called us Little and Large once.
Psycho	Yeah – once!
Homerun	Perce is the strong silent type. I'm the friendly chatty one. Small but persuasive. Sometimes punters try it on because of my size. If they get nasty or just won't see reason, a quick grab behind the door and I introduce them to Mr Baseball Bat. Whoosh! It's another home run.
Psycho	Three strikes and they're out. Ha, ha!
Homerun	Quiet tonight, Perce. No problems
Psycho	Early yet.
Homerun	Reckon it's that Bobby Brewster bloke. He's a pillock.
Psycho	Right.
Homerun	He's got them doin' that sack race thing again.
Psycho	Yeah?
Homerun	Four couples in huge sacks. First to get into each others clothes is the winner. Remember those two that were in there for most of the night?

Psycho	I do.
Homerun	They've got no sense, these kids. And those wet T-shirt competitions. If their mothers could only see 'em.
Psycho	Toga parties.
Homerun	Vicars and Tarts.
Psycho	Dirty Doctors and Naughty Nurses.
Homerun	One garment only.
Psycho	Kari bloody oaky.
Homerun	All in the pursuit of pleasure.
Psycho	All for the sake of fun.
Homerun	We've seen it all Perce.
Psycho	Right enough.
Homerun	Hey up!

The lads approach

Homerun	Evenin' lads. You alright tonight?
Brian	Fine thanks!
Homerun	Been on the ale have you?
Jason	Well just a few.
Homerun	Well take it steady then. Don't want to have any silliness or messes to clean up do we.
Brian	We'll be OK. No problems.
Homerun	Right, go on then. Have fun but be sensible.
Psycho	And don't get into trouble!
Kevin	We've got the message Squire.

They go in

Homerun	On holiday by the look of 'em. They'll be on the prowl tonight. Sometimes this place is just like a bloody cattle market if you ask me.
Psycho	True enough Charlie. Still, it's what they're here for in't they.

Scene switches to the lads inside the club. Pop music in background

Darren	Look at the place, it's heavin'.
Brian	They're four deep at the bar.
Kevin	Looks like the whole of Ferryton's here.
Darren	Loads of blokes – there'll be some competition tonight!
Kevin	For you maybe!
Jason	We'll be ages gettin' a drink.
Brian	I'll sort it. You lot find us a place. *They get ready to make a chain.*
Kevin	Right.
Brian	Here we go.

He begins squeezing his way through the 'crowd' created by the other three. Once he is through they become the lads again, gathered in a group looking on.

Brian	'Scuse me. Sorry Pal. Mind your back. Is this yours? That's OK. Right here we are. Fifty pound note should do the trick. Oi Squire. Yeah I've been here ages. Twenty pints of lager – oh – and a packet of cheese and onion please. Ta. Right here we go. Eh up. Mind your heads.

He begins to pass the beers along the chain

All	*(as the first beer arrives)* One!

They freeze momentarily

Brian	*(to audience)* Five minutes later!
All	Twenty!
Darren	Nice one Bri. Should keep us goin' for an hour or so.
Brian	What's the talent like.
Kevin	Not bad.
Jason	Those girls off the beach are here.
Darren	Where?
Kevin	Over there. Oi! Girls. Alright! Remember us? The beach!
Brian	Dead subtle Kev.

Kevin	Who cares. It's results that count. That one with the long hair. She's well tasty. I could fancy some of that.
Jason	That topless one's there!
Lads	Wahey!
Kevin	You could be in there Jase. She's alright an all. I wouldn't say no.
Brian	You never say no.
Kevin	Only live once don't you.
Jason	Not for much longer the way you're goin'.
Kevin	It's just a laugh. Isn't it. Worry too much and you won't be able to do it anyway! Got to keep your mind on the job.
Darren	On the job! Is that all it is to you?
Kevin	That's all it is to any bloke. If he tells you different he's lying.
Brian	Eh, could any of you err . . .
Kevin	What?
Brian	Be a . . . mate?
Darren	What are you on about?
Brian	You saw that girl lookin' at me on the beach?
Darren	Yeah.
Brian	Well she's here . . . and . . .
Jason	Well?
Brian	Well, I need a . . .
Kevin	What?
Brian	You know . . . a mate!
Darren	A condom?
Brian	Yeah. I thought you could lend us one.
Kevin	Lend? I wouldn't want it back would I!
Brian	You know what I mean.
Kevin	Sorry pal. Would do, but I don't use them.

Brian	But you're at it like a rat up a drainpipe.
Kevin	So? It's like washing your feet with your socks on. No thanks.
Brian	But you can't get AIDS from washing your feet can you!
Darren	Eh, Bri. They sell 'em at that big supermarket just round the corner from us.
Brian	I tried that already. It's all girls on the tills. Mind you, I'm well stocked up on anti-perspirant and plasters now.
Darren	You chickened out? There's no social stigma attached to buying contraceptives these days.
Kevin	You what? Look Bri, they've got a machine in the bogs. Just go and use that if you're so worried.
Brian	Oh right. Shit, she's lookin at me!

He starts to wriggle as if suppressing an almighty need to visit the toilet

Kevin	Bri, what the hell you doin'?
Brian	Well I don't want her to suspect anything do I. (*Loudly – almost as if in pain*) Excuse me lads but I'm burstin'!
Lads	(*unconvincingly*) Oh right, off you go then. (*etc.*)

Brian shuffles off. Scene switches to the girls

Cheryl	That's the one you fancy is it? He seems a bit weird to me!
Karen	He's just pretending that he needs the loo so that I won't think he's going to buy some condoms – that's all.
Cheryl	Oh that's all right then! I thought you'd fancy the other one.
Karen	The loud-mouthed one? Nah, not my type.
Tina	What? He's male and still breathing isn't he?
Karen	Cheeky mare!
Mandy	He seems all right to me! He's probably just showing off to his mates.
Tina	What – and really he's deep and sensitive you mean?

Mandy	Might be.
Tina	Pigs might fly and all.
Mandy	Look, I just think he's good-looking and seems good for a laugh.
Tina	Well if that's all you want. God, I mustn't drink so much tonight.
Mandy	You still can't remember anything?
Tina	Nope. Nothing. About three hours are just a blank.
Cheryl	They say your brain does that sometimes. If there's something really horrible that you'd really like to forget, your brain suppresses the memory of it.
Mandy	Wish I could forget some of the blokes I've been out with.
Cheryl	Me too.
Mandy	Remember that Trevor!
Karen	What with the breath and the hands!
Mandy	Yeah, that's the one. Eh! How do **you** know?
Karen	Let's have a dance. I like this one.
Tina	Come on then!

They get up to dance. The focus switches to the evening's DJ, Bobby Brewster.

Bobby	Hi, it's me – Bobby Brewster – your DJ for tonight here at Ferryton-on-Sea's premiere night club, 'Hollywood Nights. Coming up later we will have some Karaoke sessions and of course the grand sack race! Plus lots of fine music so we can all have a really good time tonight. And what a day it's been. Are any of you ladies out there feeling hot?
Girls	Yeah!
Bobby	And what about the guys? Are you feeling hot tonight?
Lads	Yeah!
Bobby	Then lets get you even hotter with this old favourite from Kool and the Gang – Celebration!

Music – 'Celebration'

Chorus	The night grinds on, and as the beer flows the spirits rise.
Lads	Ole! Ole! Ole! England! England! Ole! Ole! (etc.)
Psycho	Oi! Shut it! This is a night club not a bloomin football ground.

The lads be quiet

Psycho	That's better. Just remember – I've got my eye on you.
Kevin	Look come on lads. There's four of them and four of us.
Jason	Mathematical genius our Kev!
Kevin	Look, it's the only way to break them up. That Mandy has been givin' me the eye all night.
Brian	I'm game. Really fancy that Karen anyway.
Kevin	What about you two?
Jason	Suppose so.
Darren	Alright.
Kevin	Come on then.

They go over to the girls

Kevin	Evenin' girls! Remember us from the beach?
Karen	Oh yeah. Don't we.
Girls	Oh yeah, that's right. You were just next to us weren't you.
Brian	Mind if we join you

The lads all crowd in around the girls

Tina	Looks like we don't have much choice.
Kevin	Hot in here isn't it.
Karen	Very.
Brian	Yeah. Does anybody wanna drink?
Cheryl	Love one but we can't get to the bar.
Brian	Leave it to me. Same again, all round?

Pause

Chorus	The hours slip by and the drinks slip down.
	The midnight hour is passed.
	Relationships are made, broken and repaired
	But in this cauldron of heat and desperation,
	Few are built to last.

Slow music begins to play

Kevin   Wanna dance?

Mandy   Don't mind.

Brian   Do you . . . err . . .

Karen   Yeah – alright.

They get up to dance. Kevin gives a thumbs up to Brian who returns it.

Kevin   I noticed you on the beach today. Thought you looked
sound.

Mandy   Oh yeah?

Kevin   I've been waiting all night to have a dance with you.

Mandy   Me too.

Kevin   Looks like it could be our lucky night then?

Mandy   Maybe.

Kevin gives another thumbs up to Brian.

Brian   I don't believe it. She's absolutely gorgeous. Perfumes
a bit strong but she smells great. I can tell by the way
she's dancin' she's really interested. She keeps movin'
her hands all over me back. She's dancin' so close. I
can feel her right up against me. This is brilliant. I
feel . . . I feel . . . (*He is getting a little 'excited'*) Oh no!
Come on self-control. Think of something really
boring. England in the European Championships! That
usually works. It's no use. Oh god this is so
embarrassing. What am I gonna do!

Karen   Are you alright.

Brian   Oh yeah – fine

Karen   What you all twitchin' about for then?

Brian	Nothing. I'm practising the lambada that's all.
Karen	Can't you dance properly. I was enjoying it.
Brian	Me too – that's the problem. Scuse me
Karen	I'll be waiting!

He runs off. The attention shifts to Kevin and Mandy

Kevin	Where you staying?
Mandy	Some crappy old B & B. What about you.
Kevin	Sharing a caravan over at Sunnyside caravan park.
Mandy	What's it like.
Kevin	Crowded. Fancy comin' outside for a minute?
Mandy	Is a minute all you'll need?
Kevin	Depends what we get up to. Well?
Mandy	(there is a momentary pause) Yeah alright.
Kevin	Come on then. After you.

He lets her walk past him and then gives a gesture that indicates his imminent 'success' to Jason and Darren

The lights and music fade. Lights come up on Psycho and Homerun

Homerun	Well Perce, another night over.
Psycho	No trouble to speak of.
Homerun	Just high spirits most of it.
Psycho	Tried to put one lot in a taxi. They opened one door – got in. Door on the other side was open so they just carried on. Didn't have any idea where the hell they were.
Homerun	Bogs are in the usual state.
Psycho	Disgustin' isn't it.
Homerun	Fancy a quick one before you go?
Psycho	Best not. Mum will be waiting up. You know what she's like.
Homerun	Fair enough. I'll see you tomorrow then. Night Perce.
Psycho	Night Charlie.

He glares at the audience relaxes and then exits. Lights up on the lads and girls. They are gathered in separate groups on opposite sides of the stage.

Jason	Hey, where's Brian?
Tina	Where's Karen?
Darren	Gone off what that Karen!
Cheryl	Gone off with that Brian!
Kevin	Said he was taking her for a walk in that park up by the cliffs.
Mandy	Said she was going for a walk.
Jason	His lucks in tonight!
Lads	Wahey!
Tina	I hope she's careful.
Girls	Mmmm.
Kevin	I had a good time with that Mandy.
Lads	Wahey!
Mandy	I didn't do anything with that Kevin you know!
Girls	(*not believing her*) Mmmmmmm!
Jason	I don't think that Tina fancied me much.
Tina	I didn't fancy that Jason bloke.
Darren	That Cheryl could hold her beer.
Cheryl	That Darren bloke was a pathetic drinker.
Kevin	Hey – where are we?
Tina	Where are we?
All	Dunno

They all burst into drunken laughter. Lights down. Up on chorus

Chorus	So it's two o'clock in the morning
	Drunkards make their way home
	As noisily as they can.
	And in the cliff top park, looking over the broad sweep of Ferryton Bay
	Believing herself to be quite, quite alone in the world
	Just her and the still growing child

The girl comes to a desperate realisation.
And the rose tinted spectacles are shattered forever.

Jackie　　He's not coming is he. He would have been here by now. I've just been kidding myself 'cause I wanted it to be true. Perhaps he was never going to come. He just said it to keep me quiet. Perhaps he never even said it – I don't know anymore.

I don't care. I wanted it all to be perfect and it's not. But that night it seemed so . . . so much like the right time.

Lights down. Lights up on Brian and Karen

Karen　　Come on. Hurry up.

Brian　　Alright, hang on. Me shoes are full of sand!

Karen　　Well take 'em off then.

Brian　　Eh?

Karen　　Take 'em off and we'll sit down here for a bit.

Brian　　Oh yeah. All right. Great night isn't it. Look at that view!

They sit

Brian　　It's beautiful up here.

Karen　　It's dark!

Brian　　Just look at all those stars. You can't see 'em when you're down in the town. And the moon, shining on the sea. Listen you can hear the sea on the rocks. It's romantic.

Karen　　It's cold. Why don't you put your arm round me?

Brian　　Oh right, to warm you up?

He puts his arm around her.

Brian　　Hey is that someone standing over there by the edge of the cliffs?

Karen　　Where?

Brian　　Over there. I thought I saw someone.

Karen　　There's no-one there. We've got the whole world to ourselves. Just you and me.

They kiss gently as the lights switch back to Jackie.

Jackie   And he held me because I was cold and we stood there listening to the waves. I felt so peaceful. So cosy. So loved. I just wanted it to go on like that. And he kissed me and I felt warm inside as well then. When I looked at him, I knew what he was thinking, I knew what he wanted.

Switch back to Brian and Karen. Karen is on top of Brian. They are kissing passionately. Karen sits up and begins to move her hands to unbutton his trousers.

Brian   No, wait a minute I . . .

Karen   It's all right I've got plenty of condoms

Brian   It's not that, it's . . .

Karen   (*giggling*) I'll even put it on you if you like!

Brian   No wait. (*More sharply*) I said wait! Look get off me will you?

Karen   (*stopping. Puzzled and annoyed*) All right. (*She gets off him. He gets up*) What's up? Don't you fancy me all of a sudden?

Brian   Of course I fancy you. You're gorgeous.

Karen   Look, if you've got a problem then we'll take it a bit more slowly and . . .

Brian   I'm fine – it's just . . . Look why don't we just sit here for a bit and talk . . .

Karen   Talk! What about? We don't know anything about each other!

Brian   Well then wouldn't you like us to get to know each other better?

Karen   Look you fancy me don't you? I fancy you – what more is there to know? Come on!

Brian   Doesn't it bother you?

Karen   What is this? Are you a virgin or something? You might have said!

Brian   Of course I'm not. It's just well – I . . .

Karen   (*frustrated*) What?

this all you want – a quick screw on the cliff top ‌n back to your mates?

‌‌ I get it. You want a little romance don't you? You want this to be the start of a 'relationship' don't you. All this crap about the moon and stars. Well I'm not interested in that. But I really fancy you so let's have some fun.

Brian   Doesn't it bother you?

Karen   No. I just want fun that's all. And if it doesn't bother me why should it bother you? Come on – this is the last time that I'm offering.

Brian   What if you get pregnant?

Karen   Then I'll deal with it.

Pause

Brian   Come on I'll walk you home

Karen   You time wasting little prat.

She stands and adjust her dress

Brian   Sorry

Karen   (*sneering*) What will you tell your mates?

They stand looking at each other

Jason   (*in the darkness*) So how far did you get?

Kevin   (*in the darkness*) What all the way! You lucky sod.

Darren   (*in the darkness*) What was she like Bri?

Lads   (*in the darkness*) Wahey! Nice one Brian, nice one son, nice one Brian, now let's shag another one!

Brian   Nothing. Come on.

As they exit he goes to put his arm around her

Karen   Don't. Just don't.

They exit. The lights switch

Jackie   Trust me he said. It will be alright. Trust me.

Only it's not all right. He didn't mean a word of it. He only said it so he could have me. He didn't care. And it wasn't lovely and beautiful. It hurt and I cried but I told him it was, because it was so wonderful. Afterwards, I wanted him to hold me and look at the sea but he wanted to get back to his mates.

The sea. It's beautiful tonight. Glittering under the stars. It looks so peaceful. I've been so stupid. How can I face them? They'll treat me like an idiot, like a child. But I'm not. I'm not. And the shouting, and the arguments. But here it's still calm. This is my place. It would be so easy to stay. Just one step, then another. The wind in my face. It feels so clean. It makes me feel free. Like a bird. Just one more . . .

She slowly steps towards the edge of the cliff. Mrs Higgins enters behind her

Mrs Higgins	Be careful there love.
Jackie	(*stopping*) Who? What? Who are you?
Mrs Higgins	Mrs Higgins. Margaret. I couldn't help but notice that you were very close to the edge there. It can be dangerous up here. Sometimes the ground gives way. You might fall.
Jackie	I . . . What are you doing here?
Mrs Higgins	I'm just out walking. I often walk out here late at night. Can't sleep you see.
Jackie	Oh.
Mrs Higgins	Me and Frank used to walk up here a lot when we first moved here. 'Nothing like a bracing sea breeze' he used to say.
Jackie	Frank?
Mrs Higgins	Oh, my husband of course. You wouldn't know. He's dead now. God rest his soul.
Jackie	I'm sorry.
Mrs Higgins	All his life he wanted a bungalow with a nice garden by the sea. So two years after he retired we came here. Uprooted ourselves from where we'd lived all our lives to spend the rest of our days quietly by the sea

together. Well that was the plan. Never a bit of ill health in his life, then six months after we move he has this heart attack you see. At least it was quick. Almost two years ago that was. I've tried to keep going but it's hard you know. It's so lonely without me friends and I miss him so much.

Jackie   I'm really sorry.

Mrs Higgins   I would be happier talking if you came away from that edge.

Jackie looks out to sea and down at the rocks then backs up

Jackie   All right.

She slowly moves away from the edge breathing hard, realising what she was about to do

Jackie   (*awkwardly*) Hello!

Mrs Higgins   (*relieved*) Hello love. What's your name?

Jackie   Jackie.

Mrs Higgins   Nice to meet you. (*Pause*) We even had the roses around the door and the ducks up on the wall. I hated them but to Frank it was almost like an award to show that he had got what he deserved. Oh he was a good man. I loved him so much. I still do.

Jackie   Were you really just out for a walk?

Mrs Higgins   (*pause*) I suppose not. But I saw you there and – to be honest – I didn't feel like taking turns.

They laugh quietly

Mrs Higgins   Would you have stopped if I hadn't called out?

Jackie   I don't know. I don't think so.

Mrs Higgins   Are things really that bad?

Jackie   Seems like it. (*Telling someone for the first time*) I'm pregnant.

Mrs Higgins   Frank and I couldn't have kids. Always wanted them but he never blamed me. Said that I was all that he ever wanted.

Jackie   He sounds a lovely man.

Mrs Higgins	Oh he was. He was. (*Pause*) How old are you?
Jackie	Sixteen . . . well fourteen and a half.
Mrs Higgins	Your very young to be thinking of ending it all. Where's the father?
Jackie	I don't know. Don't care.
Mrs Higgins	We're a funny pair aren't we!
Jackie	Yeah.

They stand side by side looking out to sea. We hear a wave

Jackie	It must be late.
Mrs Higgins	Almost dawn
Jackie	I'm cold

Pause

Mrs Higgins	Do you fancy a cup of tea? The bungalow's not far.
Jackie	That'd be nice.

Music plays 'You Get What You Give'. Jackie walks closely to Mrs Higgins who takes her hand. As they exit Jackie leans her head on Mrs Higgins shoulder and Mrs Higgins wraps her arm around her. Music fades.

Chorus	The time and tide moves on
	And as the street lamps wink out
	The day in Ferryton draws to its close
	Some found love
	Some lost it
	Some rediscovered their childhood
	Some enjoyed just being children
	But everyone
	Found something.
	In Ferryton-on-Sea
	Ferry Town
	In these small hours
	Just before the dawn
	Hush and you can hear it breathe
	Listen
	Listen

Three waves break on the beach as the light fades. Underneath the waves we can just hear as a whisper:

Chorus Eight streets back from the sea front lies Grosvenor Road, along which comes the morning's first milk float. In the front of which, sits Mr Eastwood – Vic Eastwood. Known to his friends – and to himself in his fantasies – as Clint.

STAGING AND PERFORMANCE MATERIALS

The Last Resort can be presented in a variety of ways to suit the needs of particular groups. It was originally conceived, however, to provide an opportunity for performers to flex the wings of their imagination and create both characters and locations with a minimum of set, props and costume. The speed of the piece and the swift movement from place to place demands a flexible set with as few obstructions as possible. The action should flow from one scene to another with the changes forming part of the presentation rather than interrupting it.

Originally, The Last Resort was presented on a proscenium arch stage with a small apron. Drapes concealed the off-stage areas in the wings and the rear of the stage was covered with a large cyclorama. In front of the cyclorama there was a raised area which was dressed to represent the promenade complete with railings and lampposts. From the lampposts were strung 'party lantern' type lights. These lights, together subtle lighting changes on the cyclorama, were used to suggest the changing time of day, from dawn, through the day, sunset, night-time (with the party lights illuminated) and back to the dawn again. Although the 'prom' was used in some parts of the play, effectively this area served as a backdrop against which the main action of the play took place.

In front of the 'prom' folding chairs were placed. These chairs were the only significant props used in the entire play. The actors sat in the chairs when not actively performing and remained visible to the audience as they too observed the play. Down stage of the chairs was a large open area which could be accessed easily by the performers. This was the main performance area and took up most of the space.

This space was divided in three areas by the use of carefully focused lighting to give performance areas at Stage Left, Centre Stage and Stage Right. When combined these allowed the whole of the performance space to be evenly lit. Backlighting was particularly important for this area to effectively 'cut out' the performers from the background. An additional blue wash was used as the action moved into the night-time, and some disco style lighting was used for the 'clubbing' scenes. Transitions, when performers moved from one location to another, were marked by a change to colourful but subdued lighting and the use of music. Blackouts were not used.

The only other props were the shopping trolleys used in the 'surfing' scene. In terms of costume again the advice is to keep it as simple as possible. To create a seaside atmosphere the cast were dressed in plain shorts, T-shirts and deck shoes. To avoid it looking too chaotic, a limited range of primary colours for these costumes were used. There were no costume changes to support characterisation – all of that had to come from the actors' physical and vocal performance skills.

It would of course be possible to stage The Last Resort very differently from that outlined above. Any approach that is used however should enable the pace of the piece to be maintained and keep breaks in the action to a minimum. Plunging your audience into darkness every few minutes to cover a costume or scenery change is not advisable!

PERFORMANCE EXERCISES

These exercises are intended to help introduce a performance group to The Last Resort and some of the demands that it is likely to place upon them. For all these exercises it is assumed that the whole cast is working together in a suitable space such as a drama studio or the performance space itself.

Exercise 1

In The Last Resort the cast are required to switch between a variety of characters very swiftly. They also have to move around the stage area and set up scenes in 'neutral' – showing they are simply moving from one place to another while playing no particular role. Movement in the transition state will usually be accompanied by music and demands efficiency and focus from the performer. This exercise will help to make this clear and can also be used as a pre-show exercise to help focus the group.

a) Each person stands in a space. While standing in this space they choose another space that they are to walk to – their target. Once instructed to begin they should walk directly to their target. If another person is to cross their path they may stop and wait for them to move before proceeding. They must not alter their pathway to their target.

Once they reach their target, they pause, choose a new target and
then proceed to it in the same way as before.

b) Repeat the exercise as above only this time each participant is
carrying a chair. When they reach their destination point they are to
place their chair on the floor as silently as possible. They then look
around and select another chair and walk towards it in order to repeat
the exercise. If someone reaches their chosen chair first then they may
pause, select a new target chair and then continue with the exercise.

c) Repeat the exercise above only this time it is accompanied by a
suitable piece of music (choose something with a strong 4/4 beat).
As the members of the group perform the exercise they should pick
up and reflect the beat in their movements.

Exercise 2 – Soundscapes

The Last Resort relies heavily on the use of recorded music and
movement to punctuate the action and mark scene transitions.
Individual sound effects, however, can be created by the cast
themselves. The helicopter sounds, for instance, were made by
members of the chorus slapping their chests with their open palms.

a) The cast can be divided up into groups of four or five. Each
group is then given the title of a specific location which they have to
'capture' in sound. They may use their voices and bodies or interact
with their immediate environment (for example, by scraping chairs
or using the floor as a drum). They are not allowed to utilise anything
they would not have automatically in the performance situation.

The groups should then be given about 20 minutes to prepare
their soundscape. It can then be presented to the rest of the group.
The rest of the group should close their eyes while the piece is
performed and then be encouraged to guess the 'location' at the end
of each performance.

Suggested locations could include: A busy market place, a tropical
rain forest.

b) To extend this idea you can go on to include 'events' within the
locations such as a storm in the rain forest or a theft in the market
place. If you use voices (as voices) in these events, the voices should
be 'suggested' rather than use actual words.

c) Finally the groups should give some thought to the visual performance of the piece. As well as the sounds, they will have to perform the piece in a way that is stimulating and interesting to the eye as well as the ear.

Exercise 3 Physicalisation

In the original production of *The Last Resort*, the chorus formed themselves into a physical representation of the sea front, forming the shape of the headlands, beach and pier with their bodies, when describing the resort in the opening section. We also used physicalisation at other points to add visual interest to the scene or simply to provide a quick and a flexible means of suggesting locations.

To experiment with this idea you can play the game of 'Props' where, in groups, the cast has to form themselves into various objects.

a) Divide the cast into groups of five to six. The leader calls out the name of the object and then the groups have one minute to make themselves into a suitable shape. At the end of the minute the leader calls out 'freeze' and the groups remain frozen in place while the leader inspects them. Suggestions for suitable objects include: an iron, a food mixer, Blackpool Tower.

Exercise 4 Mime

The use of mime features heavily in *The Last Resort*. The mime used is a type of demonstrative physical style which accompanies normal dialogue and vocalised sound effects.

The style combines exaggerated characterisation with clear physical movements to suggest locations and actions which can be almost like a 'living cartoon'. The physical actions are often 'enhanced' with vocalised sound effects in much the same way that sound accompanies physical actions in martial arts films to create a 'super real' effect. In the 'surfers' scene in *The Last Resort* for instance, when the surfers mime doing up the zips on their wet suits they say 'zip' whilst doing so (emphasising the zzzzzz). Once this is done they then make a schlurping noise and suck themselves in (showing the constructing nature of the wet suits) and then sigh breathing out with an 'aaahh' as they adjust and become more comfortable.

The following exercises should help to introduce some of the necessary techniques and ideas.

ai) Each member of the group should stand in their own space and make sure that they are not facing anybody else. They should imagine that they are standing in front of the work surface in a kitchen. They should take a moment to visualise where items such as the fridge, cooker and cupboards are in relation to themselves. The should then mime the making of a simple sandwich.

The emphasis here should be on precision and exactness. If they place something on a table it should be in exactly the same place when they pick it up. Everything that they place on that table should be at exactly the same height.

aii) Having performed this exercise a few times they should then introduce sounds. Every single action should be accompanied by a vocal sound effect. Their aim is produce a clear pattern of movement and sound that can be read instantly by an observer.

aiii) Team up with a partner and show each other your exercises. Agree on just one of the exercises and develop it as a mirror exercise with one person standing in front of the other and reflecting the actions back.

b) In pairs, play a game of 'Guess the mime'. In this exercise one person chooses a scene from a famous movie or television programme. Their partner must try to guess the answer.

c) Again in pairs, imagine that you are having a conversation in a very noisy pub or club. The conversation is carried out in mime – the aim being to make it absolutely clear what you have been doing despite the absence of words. Have a clear subject, such as a job interview, rather than a generalised subject matter.

Exercise 5 Characterisation

To play roles such as the seagulls and donkeys effectively, it is good to envisage them as humans and then mix the human and animal qualities together.

The seagulls are essentially almost psychopathically aggressive – improvise a scene in which a group of skinheads constantly taunt and try to intimidate each other without ever quite coming to blows. Then add onto that a seagull like head movement and walk – soon the seagull characters will be established!

The donkeys on the other hand, are more like taciturn elderly Yorkshire men sat on a park bench deriding all that they see, and then getting up to occasional childish bouts of mischief! In the original production we simply turned three chairs so that their backs were to the audience and the performers knelt up on these, holding on to the chair backs for support. Effectively they acted the neck and heads of the donkeys only. Their conversations were interspersed with bouts of laughter that developed into brays and snorts!

Conversely, it can help with some of the more bizarre human characters, to envisage them as animals. Nelly Crabtree can be played as a scuttling turtle occasionally craning her neck out to see the world around her. Mr Minesweep can be seen as a mongoose scurrying round the stage, becoming alert and upright on making a discovery before dropping quickly to dig at the sand. Psycho can be seen as a tethered rhino always on the verge of charging head first into the fray. Rosy and Sonny could be played as rather awkward gangly giraffes!

a) In groups improvise a simple scene of a family at dinner. Each member of the group should have a distinct role in the family group. Once established the groups should begin their improvisation again. This time the group leader calls out the name of animals that they have to become whilst improvising. The content and dialogue of the scene should remain the same but the physicality and behaviour should take on the quality of the selected animals.

Suggested 'families' would include lions, gorillas or penguins.

b) In rehearsal the actors can be asked to envisage their characters as animals. They should be encouraged to observe their chosen animal either in real life or on film to avoid relying on cliché and stereotype.

They should then play a chosen scene trying to get as much of the animal behaviour into the scene as possible. They can then refine their performance until they are playing the scene as humans but with the 'quality' of their chosen animal. This can result in some very interesting and imaginative pieces of effective characterisation.

Note: There are only a very limited number of 'realistic' characters in *The Last Resort*. The vast majority of roles call for a heightened form of performance. In performance it should almost be as if the colours are a little too bright and the contrast a little too sharp.

Exercise 6 *Language*

There is a considerable variety in the forms of language used in the play. At times some of the chorus speeches are almost poetic in character, other speeches involve heightened 'dramatic' delivery or are extremely naturalistic in tone. The play is very demanding on vocal technique. Good vocal warm up exercises and general encouragement to experiment with vocal delivery should be practised.

In the chorus sections of the script, there are no indications of how the speeches are shared amongst the cast. This is to allow the maximum flexibility for performance. In the original production each line of speech in the chorus was taken by a different speaker. Sometimes two or three actors would share a passage between them. Some of the longer pieces – such as the opening – were shared by the whole cast. What is important here is to ensure that the overall sound is continuous and flowing.

a) An ideal practise speech 'off text' for chorus work is Lewis Carroll's 'Jabberwocky'. Divide the cast up into groups of four and give them a verse each from the poem. Allow them time to work together on how best to present their verse to the others. The interest needs to be developed from their vocal delivery – not their physical performance. They should experiment with sharing the lines in different ways and perhaps delivering some sections together.

The verses can then be performed, shared and discussed.

The Last Resort – The Last Word!

Exploring, rehearsing and performing *The Last Resort* should be lots of fun! Use of music copiously in rehearsal and finishing rehearsals with a dance, can be extremely beneficial and enhance group dynamics and identity – honestly (I heard you groan!).

Whenever I have staged *The Last Resort* it has always been remembered with affection by both performers and audiences. Have fun – but make it serious fun! Oh . . . and don't forget to go to the seaside!